THE ROPE-MAKER'S TALE

Other poetry titles by W. H. New

Science Lessons
Raucous
Stone/Rain
Riverbook & Ocean
Night Room
Underwood Log
Touching Ecuador
Along A Snake Fence Riding

The Rope-Maker's Tale

୭ଇ

W. H. NEW

OOLICHAN BOOKS
LANTZVILLE, BRITISH COLUMBIA, CANADA
2009

Copyright © 2009 by W. H. New. ALL RIGHTS RESERVED. No part of this publication may be reproduced, stored in a retrieval system, or transmitted, in any form or by any means, without prior written permission of the publisher, except by a reviewer who may quote brief passages in a review to be printed in a newspaper or magazine or broadcast on radio or television; or, in the case of photocopying or other reprographic copying, a licence from ACCESS COPYRIGHT, 6 Adelaide Street East, Suite 900, Toronto, Ontario M5C 1H6.

Library and Archives Canada Cataloguing in Publication

New, W. H. (William Herbert), 1938-
The rope-maker's tale / W.H. New.

Poems.
ISBN 978-0-88982-252-8

I. Title.

PS8577.E776R66 2009   C811'.54   C2008-907691-5

We gratefully acknowledge the financial support of the Canada Council for the Arts, the British Columbia Arts Council through the BC Ministry of Tourism, Small Business and Culture, and the Government of Canada through the Book Publishing Industry Development Program, for our publishing activities.

Published by
Oolichan Books
P.O. Box 10, Lantzville
British Columbia, Canada
V0R 2H0

Printed in Canada

For Peggy, Gareth, and Violet,

because the road has wings—

There will be a war, the king told his pregnant wife.
In the last phase seven of us will cross
the river to the east and disguise ourselves
through the farmlands.
We will approach the markets
and befriend the rope-makers. Remember this.

—Michael Ondaatje, *The Story*

Rope (fr. OE *rāp*), n., a cord made from twisted fibres or strands of sisal, cotton, hair, etc.; a lasso; a hangman's noose; *know the ropes*, to be familiar with a situation; v., to fasten, border, catch; *rope in*, to deceive.

Draw round.

Listen.

*There is a history
to everything,*

*and every thing
is a history*

*of water,
birth and disguise.*

Who do you think you are?

Ask: Who is this at the window, tracing
circles on the frosted glass,

child on a step-stool, old man in a chair?

*Maybe you see
only the finger moving, the ring*

*unconscious:
presentiment, a braided river near—*

*or afterthought, drawn
round—*

൞ ൙

1
FAIRGROUND

I tell you only what they told each other, the Travellers:
true or not I cannot say,

nor is it up to me to judge—I am only an ordinary
rope-maker, winding coils under the apple tree—

that is all—

What do you think you see—menace?

in cocklebur and a tangle of rags?—
I cannot hurt you—no—

my back is bent now,
breath as short as capillaire, arms

ache,
and both hands cramp from plaiting—

who do you think you see?—

maybe a wizened figure,
cider-tongued and prattling,

maybe no-one:

easy to pretend you do not notice,
walking on—

do you pay attention
to the red ants at your ankles,

the white noise of grass,
the yellow rage of a sunflower seed?

Or maybe you think you do not know me,
but you do:

I've heard you imitate uniqueness, dream your
shadow, step on cinder all year long—yes,

gather friends and scatter them,
desire and deny—

and I have craved what you have craved, thirsted
with you, laboured, blundered, tasted shame,

and twisted into hazard
every draught of ale and air—

I am old, old as rope itself, I've
occupied this shade for generations,

and I know you, watched you
scrap, scramble, crowd the city gate,

clamour to empty your leather case
before it fills again, or sell those

half-glazed pots you carry with you,
sullen with certainty—

yes—

Skirting the hangman's house
and tramping the dust in williwaws,

you're not the first to walk this road,
nor likely the last, if you listen—

Draw round:

do you hear the dun sound of muffled bells?

a carousel already starts to turn—

I tell you
I have seen the Travellers:

Listen:

୨୨ ୧୧

I tell you
only what they said along the way,

after that time when the last bell rang
and the wings flew

and the war destroyed the city
and seven fled:

the **Man** (still young, though he'd be old before the
  end);
his pregnant **Wife**, with snakeroot powder, ginseng,

leaves of the fingerplant, needle, angelica,
pennyroyal, thread;

her stern Friend the **Waterwoman**
and the ponderous **Keeper**, the porter of keys,

she as thin as silence, drifting shadow,
he pitching backwards, pouched with opinion;

and still three more: **Landsman, Gambler, Actor**—
one a giant, dark-browed, dour,

one impulsive, red-haired, small, the last like
maize and fire, silken, restless, air—

I tell you only what they said to me: *history*
is water,

and water a history of frozen moments
meeting, evaporating,

rigid, rapid, ignored.

Until you hear them.

Cycling.

Over time.

I saw the Travellers long before they reached me
and asked for safety—

heard their voices on the wind,
read the darkness,

caught glimpses in the teeming face of others
who swore that safety lay within these walls

yet wandered riverwide, tenaciously,
around their own preoccupations—

I saw them:
listen—they spent years

gathering distance
and packing it away,

tenting when they could,
overnighting otherwise on rocky headland,

out of reach of dragons' teeth
and arrows—

Being human, they lied,

and therefore lived:

to draw figures, tell me tales,
and counsel what they reckoned they believed.

    Whatever is true, said one,
    or useful, said another,

    or fun, said the **Boy**,
    who was born along the way—

    or easy to sell, the glittering **Merchant** murmured,
    when halfway along he stood before them, trinkets in
       hand,

    *tin pans, talismans, gods and guarantees, all
    wrapped in story*—

Silence: and then

    or worthy, says the Landsman:

૭ ૭

But it's the Merchant who speaks first
when the Travellers reach the Fairground—

when uproar assails them, bits of ash
thrash the air, and once again the Boy says

Tell me a story—

the Merchant who speaks first,
murmuring to himself before he speaks aloud,

wondering

> *How much will they believe—*
>
> *and do I want them to?*
>
> *Do they ever stop to ask, when they stop to listen?*

He knows the Midway's crowded, that sunhats
and pickpockets jostle cotton shifts and breeches,

that colour draws, and speed distracts:
that noise is necessary

to confusion.

Street-slick and glassed against the sun,
he knows his territory,

and while he walks
he calculates the pace of his approach:

It's not just speed and the tearaway rides, but how the ring-vendors tease and taunt—how we promise something-for-nothing, or at least something, ANY thing beyond the furbelows of sunday, even the colour of ghosts. We're canny, we are, selling the face of possibility—

So the kewpie dolls we promise along the Strip make a flimsy sense, stuck in their grins. Touts and shills wear progress like a guarantee, swallowing cash and smiling. We hardpeddle miracles, we do, perform enthusiasm as though we believed it's real— EVERYONE'S A WINNER FOLKS, TEN FOR A DOLLAR & SHOOT FOR A WIN, YOU CAN'T PRESS UNLESS YOU IM-PRESS—and oh yes, the darts are blunted, the diamondback balloons are underblown, we know, we know, we say AHH, TOO BAD, KID, TRY AGAIN, and they do, they do—

☙❧

COME-ON-IN! he shouts, inviting the Travellers into the chute.

COME-ON-IN: *it's just a little fall, what can hurt you in a little fall—your weariness, my friends, give yourself a break from all your weariness—toss away*

*those masks you wear, those cowls that cover you,
it's easy, feel the summer on your back—look at the
youngsters here, they love it, you can do it, you de-
serve it, you're secure!*

൞൜

He knows how falling appeals, loss

and raw desire: the power of suspense,
the attraction of the dare: in-

tensity before—duration, delay—
then after, giddy relief, so—*EVERYONE'S*

A WINNER—they will circle back for more.
It's in between when the terror falls—

when they surrender to the skeins
of un-control. They think of it as action,

but all's illusion on the Fairground here,
including their dream of safety.

The moment they reach for a nickel
they're stirring the anger in danger,

the vulnerable zero always in love—

And so what if they think they can rise above their nakedness on narrow rails and patented designs, rub away the boundaries that fix the earth in place, forge an empire out of speed? So what if physics'll force the riders home and after all they'll fail to fly—so what? They're never far from a ticket booth: a clutch of loose change and once again they're emperors of air: for ONLY A DOLLAR, defiant joy— nothing for it but to start again—

COME-ON-IN!

You see those sideshow barkers strutting the boards in candystripes and straw hats—

COME-ON-IN!

those bearded ladies, swinging tassels, dancing bears, and universal truths they sell?

They're all one, to me, the lit-up scent of money— everything candyfloss and mustard, witching rods and maps of the magic East. The Midway thrives on this thicket of need: for puppetry and freaks, peep shows and lucky breaks, one chance to be sovereign and never weep again—women pregnant with hope at the river's edge, men riding anxiety all the way to cover, laughing and laughing and putting their money down on a tin Utopia—

But do I tell them? do I hell—

❧❦

Wide-eyed, the Boy
listens.

Why do you suppose?

because all stories spin adventure,
and spiders thrive on tangled trails?—

because the Merchant needs a listener,
and even a child will do?—

or is it because the others are tired,
have travelled so long

they need reprieve
from threats in the night:

threats that have harried them
like unpronounceable names,

like the fingernails of ghosts
and the claws of mottled rats,

like the poisonman with liquid lullabies,
the maker of clocks who collected hands—

hair rises on the backs of their necks,
the wind hisses *serpent* in the undulating dunes—

Are you listening?

Come—closer—
draw in—

II

THE RUSH OF WINGS

Some people said later it was a gold ring
that started the story, others the war itself.

But the Old Man (who was old before his story
ended, though not when it began, so many years

before) always swore it was the insect wings.

Wings the height of a tall man's knee, he said.
Suddenly there in the stone lane, early as rubble,

late as rags, and raw as sawtooth
after the war had lagged for a generation

and plague had killed the old ones
who thought they would live forever

and rats laughed
and the night of ice that had fallen fast

now never seemed to end.

It was then, he said, then

that he slipped from the shell that used to be
his father's house, then that he scuffed through

castoff bodies, looking for water, then that the night
shivered, and the insect wings began to fly:

they led him toward the river, he said, away
from ague spears and the acid pool: it was then

that he heard the last bell crack in the east gate,
and a voice declaimed *seven times seven, the child*

*will be a boy: if you would see him live, go. Follow
the ring road. See if it will lead you to the moon—*

ೞ ೲ

That was *Then.*

I heard this long ago, on a day of cindergrit and salt,
drawing a thread from an osier basket

just like this—shaking off scorpion
and bramblethorn and twisting it secure—

That was before my hands knotted,
when I was young, and I thought the voices dream—

But then there's
After then:

It's always *After then*
that alters a journey's end.

So with the Travellers,
Hope and horsehair, sisal and rag.

❧

Would you prefer a straight path?
hand-rail, hemming-wall, cobbled market square,

no branch, no gap, no ciderscented tree?
or do you dawdle

in the coils of unpredictability,
the brownbottle spin of indirection—

❧

You might guess the Man left the city,
his pregnant Wife with him; the Waterwoman

who was her friend; Landsman, Gambler,
Keeper of keys—would-be helpers all—

and the Actor, whistling fire, whispering air.
You might guess

they left the war behind as they expected to,
along with the broken house and the old country—

disguising themselves in rough cloth and sandals,
to start—

they tied cord around their bodies, covered their heads,
and called themselves pilgrims when anyone challenged—

as many did: fire-breathers
whom the playful Actor flattered,

wrestlers
whom the giant subdued,

sentries and skeletons,
sorcerers and drones:

all dangerous, all fierce, all had to be
outwitted, puzzled, distracted, confused—

the Gambler quick, the Wife assured, the Waterwoman
casting umber among the shadowless—

so they fled the plague of rats, slipped
out of the city, climbed into the Eastern hills:

yet for miles on end the Man looked back,
till the gate disappeared into sky,

and the past, like the land, became foreign—

> *After my father died,* he murmurs, only half aloud,

> we gave away the uniform—the brass buttons, stripes,
> and all that khaki.

The heather my mother knit in other years (dreaming
high country, burn and moor) had long since unravelled,
and the boots worn through.

She'd seen the northland only once: for her it lived in
ritual, first foot and crooning. She sipped from a thistle-
patterned cup, yes. And opened doors,
until the end.

The guns were a different story—

and told other stories: targets, rounds of ammuni-
tion—the splay of possible bodies whispered away from
children's eyes. Though what could she do about the can-
nons. Some

countries

no longer exist. Their people stilled. By absence, the curi-
ous shell of khaki and brass. Only the old

call out

the colour of ghosts.

I must move on—

Yes—but ring roads curve in circles,
and the moon wanes.

The Man tries to lead, of course—*The voice spoke to ME*,
he says, more often than is helpful—and the others

go along, not irresistibly for good, but keen to survive
for now, and they balk less than you might have thought,

for each has a way of saying aloud
how they read the world.

> *Custom and habit, progress and change,*
> *random uncertainty, seventh heaven.*

While in the silence of their minds
lie the tales they tell themselves,

to worry fear.

I heard them all.

I heard the Gambler with his lucky pennies,
tallying signs on the morning roadway:

> *a dead skunk,*
> *a gunny sack,*
>
> *a broken*
> *black umbrella:*

And I heard the Keeper of the keys reply:

*If I were a betting man, and of a Revelations
mind, I'd guess the seventh seal was about to break,
the silent angel soon to close the book: I might sell
reliquaries, cast bent ribs and banded animals*

*as omens of seven-sin reprisal, protection lost
against the wormwood skies while Tigris flames
and old Euphrates rages, blood and blood
and bleeding—I'd say the stink of decay*

*is our only inheritance—ashes and sackcloth
all we have to bequeath—what are we
doing here, I'd ask. But I am skeptic, posing why
by quarryside, seeking sure alternatives—*

*Signs are what the mind reads, not messages
from morphine and the dead. Though the rivers
we cross run scarlet. Though clinkers fog the sky.
Though the amber desert extends, extends—*

ಌ ಌ

The others choose not to react, or at least not
face to face. I do not tell you what I do not know,

for who can make rope without sweet grass, jute,
the weaver's art and strings? Can you hear the bells they

dream about, stumble on their boulders, smell the burning
where the dragon flares? Mostly their minds

fix upon flight, and on the child about to be born,
keeping him safe, and the Mother-to-be.

Singularities.

But she—
she finds seventy ways to truth,

luminous moonstones to read against the dark:

> *madness,* her sibyl says, *cycling round the eyes,*
> *iris staring into ice, wheeling certainty*
> *or un-, the fixity of pestilence and war.*

It might be a question—

> *madness,* she says, *the ratwheel of history,*
> *cage within cage, the whirr in the mind's ear*
> *as loud as missile hits and detonation.*

Or maybe she's outfacing fate,
seeking hope for the Boy—

or a quiet of her own—
for does she hear *madness*?

or does she hear wide-eyed laughter,
a way to live in the face of living?

৯৫

The men ignore her. Oh, they think they are
being solicitous. No doubt. But they do not listen,

not for any length of time. They make camp,
they break camp, they fashion tools, they

hide their traces—
they have to solve things, the men believe,

while the moon moves on.

And all the while, distance becomes an ocean,
with surfaces they do not recognize

and hollows they haven't supposed.
This will be home, they say, and then

Not home at all, there are no footprints here,
creating them, erasing as they go.

Everywhere sand shifts beneath them, mud entraps,
the sun endangers them, the heat restores:

night and rain and rain and darkness
quench and frighten, ambush and guarantee.

Practical or not they hazard solutions,
or what they call solutions, maybe smoke

and candlewax—
like the kindling Actor,

who wears an answer on his borrowed shirt:
BRING BACK PANGAEA, as though to do so

were the same as gaining ground—

Such dreams.
Such dangerous dreaming.

For when the world starts falling apart,
drifting away in a wake of islands,

self-styled wizards take quick to the road,
their green elixirs promising what used to be—

cartographies of certitude,
boxes floating fixed atop sargasso and salal—

and they're practised in snake-oil sales, I know them,
these circuit magicians. They find plenty of people

ready to buy their poison-bottle truths,
and plenty more uncertain,

while others stand about on their tumbling rock,
tempering their bones with good intentions.

They will jump, they say, onto solid ground,
if ever uniformity should happen round again—

Well.
He was young, the flickering Actor. Give him that.

So were they all, save for two: the knotted, plodding
Keeper with his tarnished barrel keys,

and the Woman's friend—

puzzling, that one:

wrinkled as brookwater, wary,
impassive as cold. The Actor tried to avoid her.

But the Keeper they all trusted, up to a point—
when they weren't bristling at how he

circled round a thing, or when they weren't
forestalling him, or storming off, or when they

wanted a straight line away from the east gate,
and he'd murmur elliptically instead,

> *I do not seek a simple close,*
> *but how words turn, and why:*
> *what they have to do with what we call*
> *truth, or is it lying—*

III

BIRTHING, BRAWLING

When the Woman's time comes, then,
in the dark of an early morning,

they set up tents in a grassy field where
two rivers meet, and wait out the rhythms

of labour. Myself I expected them to make
more of the moment—dance, chant antiphons,

burn dragon's blood and lemon balm, dittany
and lotus: it was, I thought, what they'd been

walking for, the possibility of hope, some
faith in the elements, a future free of pain—

the Boy's, if not theirs, twisting the two together,
fraying, afraid.

Instead,
despite themselves,

they invoke the past
and all its walls of precedent and similarity: and so,

while the Waterwoman deals with need,
and the Gambler wagers on the hour,

and others sharpen tools and whittle toys
and pace the earth in eights and orbits,

the Keeper falls obliquely into proverbs,
precepts, somnolent decrees,

as though they satisfied,
as though they seeded light, showered daisies

over the birth itself, the next day,
the life to come:

> *some say Solomon pronounced the last word, and some say no,* intones the Keeper—*last words come from the barleyfield, where village women tell each other husband-truths and when the river flows, how to live with silence, how to boil soup from shoots of stone, and poison rats when the wet season comes.*

✤

> *and the schoolman fixes another truth on a calfskin page: tells us the alchemist kept a tiny devil in the pommel of his sword, and though he was a failure in science as in love, was undismayed—so who called him Bombastus? perhaps the women: likely the sword was a field story too, a metaphor of afterdark for them to laugh over under the rough chaffing of midday.*

✤

> *where are the seven pillars of wisdom: not among the foolish, say the scribes, however sweet the secrecy of stolen bread—while the women murmur into their scarves, do what you must to survive, who writes these rules but those who claim to rule.*

✤

and dead flies: they make even the healing ointments of an old apothecary stink, for the smallest of follies outlast the savour of wisdom: but the women know the sound of bluebottles humming history on the fields of war, they have heard them often, and they whisper emptiness, curse weaponry, shout anger at the ghosts and the going away.

The men mean well, I suppose,
even if their actions seem haphazard

and ruminations wild:
but I do not judge—I tell you

only what I learned from them, frost and meltwater,
yellow-tip and straw—

৩৯

For when the child cries,
and the men brake, brace, and carry on,

the Woman does not utter platitudes and maxims,
curse ferally, recite cold laws—

she summons an old and greenleaf charm
against disease, despair:

jockey vermilion, jagged and finikin,
horses do fling disobedient manes,
the filly's hooves ring TINEA, TINEA,
fingering itch and juddering pain,
itch and pain and ice and rein
and bitterweed begone:

she knows no river promises an estuary,
only the fraction of history it scours

between its shores,
and funnels irretrievably away—

൙ ൙

Maybe only her Friend the Waterwoman understands,
attending her with clean cloths and pleated singing

and stories she'd learned in a faraway childhood,
from other mothers in other times:

in villages outside Sparta, in circles of salt,
the women are threshing grain: the floor (halos,
they call it) crackles with lash and scattered
straw: they dream of flight—

✶

in the temple to Helios, artisans paint radiance,
god, with a disk of light behind his head: they
have not seen the sundogs that light an Arctic sky,
nor rings of peacock feathers in the Persian dawn,
but they have watched how emperors
have coined themselves as deities,
and they dream of flight—

✣

messengers: they wait for messengers
to bring them answers, carry them away, explain
who and why they are: eagles, ravens, vultures,
nimbus doves, each with wings extended—
or they wish on the gloriole around the moon, ice
in the troposphere, to rise, and rise again—

✣

north of Athabaska, a solitary hiker
breaks from the scrub, sweaty with canvas and summer:
around his head he wears a halo of blackflies,
writing angels into seven-painters air—

✣

which of them is holy: birdwatcher,
minotaur, thresher of the moon:
in the ring of consciousness,
they dream of flying—

I say the Waterwoman only knows. She's the one
who circles round, spins song out of silence,

shapes confidence from cry.

I could be wrong.

The Man, too, knows something,
something as gossamer as insect wings:

for he is the Woman's lover, husband, tender at times,
the father of the Boy.

He knows about the thread of life
that binds the generations,

knows it's like a messenger in war—
in jeopardy—

It strikes him dumb, this knowing—

his heart is split
between his own torn youth

and all he wants to promise
to someone new:

They come like starlings, he whispers,
missives from afar:

black marks smudged on an airweight page,
crying—

or sometimes like a flirt of chickadees
in scarlet japonica,

chittering
cowslips, a ground to spring on—

>   *You hesitate,*
>   *and then*
>
>   *hesitate,*
>
>   *before*
>
>   *tearing open the envelope,*
>
>   *asking,*
>
>   *let there be:*

colour, singing birds,
ropes of story to braid with the grandchildren—

a shawl to draw round when we're old

and cold—

clean water, bread to eat,
and on a fair day, strength to remember

the Blackfoot call of creation:
    let there be laughter—

His lips move
to the rhythms of breath.

He whispers a blessing—

    ❧ ☙

So at last, celebration: I heard them
happy, they sing lullabies, tell bogie stories,

reinvent the past and call it history, cast
knucklebones, divine what's yet to come—

They think they have achieved.

It does not last.

Without thinking, quickly they
recompose themselves in flame,

and clustering about the Boy,
begin to press upon him

all they say that he must know—

    to guarantee his future—

meaning theirs—

Their narratives dance awkwardly—old hope
tied up in weariness, old wisdom worn as doom:

the Gambler talks of sacrifice, the Man of runes,
the Actor blurts out warning lines, the Keeper

blue determination—the Boy's their future,
they believe, and (one small step) their *prize*,

so soon they argue. *Who is right?* they ask—
and answer singly, all as one, *I am, I am, I.*

∽∾

Tense:

they watch each other closely now, the past
catches them, sudden, like fire's shadow,

ghost's fingerscratch. They circle,
circle,

wary of the first strike: voices
skitter, shingle, scuffle, scorch: sound

inflates like fusillade across a pond—

Clamouring to be The Only,
they tilt for the Boy.

Cacophany.

☙☙

It hurts me still, this brawling—rattles me,
throws me off my measure—

look, I've torn the thread—
must stop,

untwist, unwind,
repair—

One at a time, then.
Sisal,

cotton,

hemp,
flax,

rag. There.

Now:

❦

If I were you, Boy, trumpets the Actor,
the Keeper planing overtop *When I was young—*

Who do you think you're talking to, the Gambler
thunders—*a stowaway of seven score?*

All the Boy needs to know is *when to act,*
he'll figure out himself the how: Listen up, I say,

> *The first time you go to a stone henge,*
> *go on a grey day, the sky overcast,*
> *light drizzle pocking the skin:*
>
> *The first time you go to a stone henge,*
> *go in the sun, shadows crisp*
> *against the blue:*
>
> *The first time you go to a stone henge,*
> *ignore the weather—go at night,*
> *go when the blackness closes in:*
>
> *The first time is the only time:*

You can't return to a stone henge,
the stones will shrink, the day
evaporate in blue or rain or grey—

Only the first is the time to see
druids circling, cloaked in intention,
each step skirting the altar, near,

knives you imagine bright and glistening,
solstice locked to a moment of light:
chanting, chanting, a chorus of dread—

but next time, only the wind—

൭ൠ

If nothing else,
these skirmishes to claim the Boy

stir the Man to speak: he has been
dreaming yet again

of life before the birth, and after:
leaf music, wishing sweet,

and then his own hands stolen from him, lying
useless on a pebbled floor, draglines

holding him, rat-men clattering glass
alleyways—or else he's caught in the cogs

of clocks, and a massive mallet's pounding
ice, ice, ice, ice, and

Fool he mutters, smarting, halt
at the steep edge of abandon.

He has to pry himself out of pause,

convince himself of what he must do,
and what he can: he grabs at things

that seem like solid facts, seizes vague
hints, circuitous reflections,

bits of story he only half remembers,
and tries to turn puzzle into fatherly advice—

and he succeeds, as all fathers do,
in sharing mostly his confusion: *You'll*

read the signs, Boy, he says—
then stumbles to explain:

    picture stones will tell you stories:
    of wandering lives, fierce battles, dragons that
    dwell in caves and fire that falls from the hills:

    in the distance the green lands, here the ice:
    and wal-knots, the rings that carry warriors
    by horse or boat to the next world—

✷

*but how to build a wal-knot is one of its mysteries: link
three rings, the masters say—my father told me this when
I was young—join them so that no one will link to any
other,*

*but take one away and all will fall apart: head, heart,
body—earth, sea, air—this world, next, the passage be-
tween: the pattern's clear, you follow?*

yes—

though I confess

I cannot craft it whole—

✷

*it's why we read the picture stones:
the icy certainty of heroes, runes of faith
and consolation—or else death—*

*though on the tiled floor of the fabled island,
and in the plausible twists of a garden of knots,
the rings still pull together hope,*

*or what we take as hope, signs of connection:
a past to hold, an earth to last, a ring of friends
to carry on. With ice in place, we say we live*

*in the green lands, not in caves: we do not fear
the dragon: all that will be is—except—
that drum of doubt: what if, what if, what then?*

IV

BOUNDARY DREAMING

I could see years pass as they fenced their stories
back and forth, parrying—and each one grows

a little older: the Gambler adds heft, the Landsman
stoops, the Actor sprouts a cornsilk beard.

They reinvent themselves elastically,
to match the landscape they travel, to persist,

they put on new hats, new coats, wear dungarees and
red bandannas, black jackets and ice-blue ties:

they try at once to claim distinctiveness
and disappear inside convention. The Man

greys visibly: his temple
pulses. The women

hide their faces from the sun.
The Keeper ages

hardly at all.
And they walk.

Walk.
In the same direction.

East.
The Actor casually. The Gambler

evenly. The Man heavily,
as though he wanted wings, while the Boy

grows as he will, without needing yet
to choose among them.

And as the land steepens,
dropping into salt flats and shell,

the men call a truce in their little war,
and together they walk on into the dry

as though nothing had changed,
stalking the moon

and whatever lay at the ring road's end—

till:

☙ ❧

till they remember the poisoned earth:

till they hear the women's silences:

till the Landsman spins alternatives
out of field and spiral:

you wouldn't think—he pauses—
*sitting lakeside on diorite—
watching the geese return north
after the ice has begun to melt—*

*or standing at creekedge in another season,
the tumble of salmon coming back to spawn,
reddening the shallow rapids—
that your mind would turn to coroners—*

*but so it will: the wonder of the moment,
the sudden need to find reasons—
beyond habit, beyond belief—for life
and death, the cycle, the logic of generation:*

*urgency, yes—desire and will—
even the food chain, chance and expectation—
but more: creekedge, lakeside,
you're wreathed in the energy of decay—*

*ponder the land if you will, and the lives
you walk among, they're as subject to blood
and hunger as you, and though discard is the way
of genes*—ADAPT OR DISAPPEAR—*continuity*

*is a dream of better, not of waste:
why then will you tolerate distortion, the poison
of quick solution? mercury runs in the water table,
snails invade, and loosestrife kills—*

Stiff, sore, exhausted, vexed,
they shuffle at the Landsman's words. I see them

slowly facing what they've fought about:
the fear they carry with them—

they fear even that they carry their fear
down every artery and home in every vein:

it poisons them.

They've come far, remember,
and coped whenever danger threatened

from without—they've lived through hunger,
the rat plague, precipice and question—

but how little they have moved: the war,
the war, the dragon war—it holds them

like hands, exposes them
on a boneyard plain. They are afraid.

Yes, they try to tell *once upon a time*
from *coming soon*—

but always the boundaryline blurs,
for what starts out as fairytale burns

incandescently to bones. Where did they learn
that compulsion, the men, to put things in order:

by which they mean fences, furrows, shells—
not just their quarrels over which direction to follow—

or who—but also quarrel's ancient carousels,
unsettling:

> *it was this side of the seventh river*
> *we met the magician, bartered flint,*
> *sold the ring: I say the other—*

yes and *no* dissolving into silences
they will not put a name to, *gruff, game,*

guard, gain, the stiff syllables of afternoon.

∽∾

They could ask themselves what the others fear.
But they seldom do.

Instead they talk their silences to me.
Or to the Boy.

Whatever they choose to say,
the Boy's entranced, drawn in.

Feigning sleep, he listens, hears—

hears *something*, he thinks—

and puts it away,
for maybe later,

while frost circles in the drowse of dark,
and other stories rise from the ember stones.

Each spring they gather at some bridge
where a county level measures depth,

and stare mutely at the water rising. Each
spring they gather where folk memory

measures danger and flow,
and toll the same stories:

> *the year the preacher lost his head*
> *and rang the steeple bells all night,*
>
> *the year they plucked the madam*
> *from the farmhouse roof*
>
> *and youngsters paddled housecats*
> *in birch canoes*
>
> *to higher ground,*
> *the year the sirens blared and the*
>
> *locksmith drowned in a tub of holy water,*
> *trying to set his goldfish free.*

That year, they say.

Meaning *this*.

Always it's really this year, the eye trying to gauge
if and when. If the floodcrest crosses the border today.

If it breaks through the sandbags. If there's anything
more, as they lean, close, at the rail.

Or when it's too late to seed.
When the crop is ruined.

When it's finally time to load the wagon,
get out of the game.

Again.

They do not exactly believe the stories they tell.
Coughing into the east, grim as persimmons.

But I hear them,
and while they jostle with each other,

year in,
year out,

and move, still moonstruck,
ridge and ridge to valley stone,

their distance keeps the dragoman alive,
the uncontrollable flood from closing in,

and I become interpreter, their ears in the world,
their ragged tongue—

൜ൡ

The Boy's Mother dreams aloud
of a past that might once have been real:

desire, romance,
or emptiness:

> Rolling somersaults at the green edge of play, chirping excitement just to be wherever wasn't ordinary, where old men in white hit centuries on oval afternoons, and came alive to break for tea. Run-up and spin. Applause scattering like grass.

✻

> I stop at the corner. A crocodile crosses the road, and suddenly time turns back on itself, blue beret and chattering teeth, I'm on the way home, and the lizard is chasing. I do not remember colour: the world is khaki, brown and grey. Where does the rainbow come from, scaling this intersection, dipping and swaying like cardboard clouds? And where does it go, when soon arrives too early on the doorstep?

✻

> We walked to town in those old black-eyed-susan days, drifted past August as though foot-soldiers were not away, corvettes at sea. In reach and still untouchable, blue shadows lean across the boundary line, peaks stark and snowfields spare in front of the dying sun.

✻

> And yet the next day dresses again as holiday, the dog swims in slippery circles, the wicket keeper dons fresh whites as though nothing grieves and flower-baskets bloom forever. The ordinary unimaginably far away, the century unimaginably near.

When the Boy hears her,
he, too, begins to sing:

> girls and boys are sad in the morning,
> sad as the moon in the year of the crow,
> cold without supper, cold without warning,
> who is the ringman, what does he know

✻

> sad as ash in the hot afternoon,
> burned from house and banished from home,
> crows in the attic, crows on the tongue,
> who is the ringman, talon and tome

*sad in the evening, sad in the night,
sad for the children, the hurting inside,
all the magicians addicted to fighting,
who is the ringman, where does he hide*

but when the Woman hears the Boy,
she weeps:

*at the playschool they're just learning colours
ring-a-rosie*

*black white the plenitude of grey,
they gather in circles, not rows,
test the strength of London Bridge,
the musicality of chairs, ring-a-rosie—*

*red yellow blue (bleu clair, says one,
pink and orange, says another),
they have their favourites,
and crayon beyond the edges of the page—*

*Simon says jump and all of them do, and then
jump and everyone laughs and they can't stop
talking about the day before when they were
little and the teacher jumped even when
Simon didn't say, ring-a-rosie—*

*what happens if they don't watch out—
someone says puce, someone says ugly,
the bridge begins to disconnect before they*

notice where they're standing
ring-a-rosie ring-a-rose—

sudden,
the noticing,

green green brown
they all fall down—

Tell me a story, says the Boy.

&

For the storyteller, it all comes down to this:
a few machinations, a perilous circle of friends,

a fantasy where good should always win—

but the power to hurt can hide in anonymity,
and tricks blow reason away—you know that glass

depends on stones—

and the Man is preoccupied.

So when they reach the Fairground—
yes, now is the time—they are divided,

ready to be distracted by the riverserpent loops,
ripe to fall for the Merchant's tongue.

COME ON IN, he says, all tassels and bears,
COME ON DOWN—

V

THE BELLS

But it's not the Boy—it's the Gambler
who rises first to the Merchant's taunt,

the enticing offer, provocation:
he is in love with numbers, plays with them,

is tempted by the draw—the shuffle of cards,
the tumble of dice, the ratchet of likelihood

slowing the wheel—
though all the Travellers are vulnerable

to what they call Experience,
the odds of a sure thing—

so when the Merchant speaks, the Gambler
hears an opportunity, takes his chance

on rolling sevens:

>*go little dies*, he says,

muttering incantations,

>*go stone the devils, meet with dragon's teeth,*
>*voyage with princes across seven tides,*
>*go where you will, but take me in hand,*
>*dance with doves through a seven-veiled sky—*

colour will greet you, shades of the rainbow:
search for the seven gold sisters of night:
candles they are, in the hold of the darkness,
picking direction in hours of flight—

talismans,
against ambush, annihilation—

↬↫

He's met others, the Gambler, with madstones and rabbit's
   feet,
and mocked them all: theosophists who praise 3, 4, 7:

light, life, and union; kabbalists who love the marriage
of 3 and 4, logos becoming tetragrammaton.

They do not bring him ease.

He's seen the codes of completion,
he says,

> *the sexes holding hands*
> *inside a perfect circle*
> *inside a perfect square inside*
> *a trinity of arms:*

but always he asks to move on—

Lucky legs, he cries, *5 and 2—*

∽∾

The others stir at the Gambler's daring—
and instantly the Fairground draws them in:

they gape at oddity, shiver at noise, then start
to drift: the Keeper seeks the fortune-teller's booth,

glimpsing crystal behind the curtain, the Actor's
fixed on fire-eaters and high-wire walkers,

the Landsman fastens on the dancing bears.

And keen to master the looping rides, the Boy
suddenly darts off, avoids the Man's stick,

the Wife's cry, the Waterwoman's arm,
and disappears along the Midway

into the quilt of colour, the river of stray.

The Merchant smiles:

Never out of sight, he tells himself, *never out of sight: the loop-the-loop twists sailors' knots out of the near horizon, paints filigree against the sky, feeds parables in motion, curls dopplers of pulsing screaming high into iron rings—*

when I watch their eyes I see them snatch fear from the steel and unsafe sky, fly distance into dreamland—up and off they go, dragooned by hope: oh yes, I can see them, they are nearly mine—

Who knows what could have happened then?

But you know, don't you—you've been there yourself, to the Fairground—

simple surrender, perhaps, to light, darkness, copper crowns, lost threads and ragged hems—

but I tell you only what they told me, of the scuttle down the Midway, the Gambler's play,

the shouts and threats and crude recriminations, the promise of control, the draw of disarray—

Pandemonium.

And then I heard the Gambler's voice rising above the rest, growling *Loss Loss* and

    Sevens From Hell!

Irate he was, at having been outfoxed,
outplayed: *They'd fixed the pawl*, he shouts,

to anyone or none,
and I did not see!

He shakes his head, tears at his sleeves, beats his
barrel chest, and stamps on both unbuckled shoes

till the stripes in his jacket twist alive
and jungle him in vines—

༄༅

Who knows how far divergence would have taken them,
scrambling after numbers they want and dancing words

they don't yet comprehend: *Safety,* they pant, and then
Wealth, Power, Fame—hurling darts and dropping coins and

weaving down haphazard alleyways—
and all the while the Merchant follows them,

reading knowingly the clutch of desperation,
the glass splinters of desire—

Who knows how far—
far as the road is round—

until the Keeper pulls away from the fortune-teller's booth
and from the conjurors who claim to speak with ghosts,

and ponderous as ever, he rumbles one of his
brooding stories slowly, speaking low,

till each of the Travellers hears his voice
and reassembles near:

choosing the right word is hardest,
the border a thin line between us and them,
or an energy of negotiation (us with them
more than them with us, size always assumes power)—

so PARALLEL, *yes, meaning beside one another,*
though that won't quite do, with angles
jutting out from all that's left of the old lines,
stranded north, where ice has melted,

as though to remind us how illogical
straight lines are on a map of movement:
PARALOGISM, *therefore, beside reason,*
though which of us possesses, is possessed—

mad, to pretend we never overlap: mad, too,
to assume we cannot see, say, touch, value
our differences—so PARALLAX *instead:*
being beside change, bringing in breath

when we need it, a second, third line,
sustaining our own momentum even as we
marvel at the other's unself-unconsciousness,
the speed of the steel blade, the spin—

it is PARALYSIS *we need to ward away—being*
loose beside—wing out of position when we
need to move ahead, coherence giving way
to random mimicry and careless faith in stars:

go down at night to the river's edge, stand by day
at the lakeshore: listen for the singing,
it's how we live, and what we live for,
the latitude to play on—

He tends to talk in circles, the Keeper does,
sometimes with such abstraction they think him wise,

at other times in strange allegories, tales they listen to
but puzzle over after, piecing meaning separately, each alone—

This time, yes,
they have again come back together,

but the Woman is perturbed when she returns;
and the Man annoyed, she with the Man's impatience,

he with the relocated Boy, and all their faces
grim. The Waterwoman's guarded, the Landsman

furrowed in distress, the Boy silent, moon-eyed
with what he's seen, while the Keeper of the keys

supposes on. The Gambler, who's been holding
at the Midway's edge, waits till the exhortation's

done, then approaches, coatless, his shirt-tails
torn and falling away, and when he does the Actor

capers, clowns about, shaking the company loose
from the Merchant's spell. *Circuses*, he crows,

are fair illusions—and laughter starts the world anew—
At once the Boy's Mother murmurs

> *Fairytale or no, a circle of friends*
> *is the only way on,*

and the Landsman adds,

> *Our journey's a plain hunt.*
> *We move because we must.*
>
> *Whenever night draws on,*
> *remember the bells:*
>
> *The first stroke breaks the silence,*
> *rushes past inertia the way sparrows*
> *scatter when shadows stir at the edges*
> *of sight. Thunder. The day changes,*
>
> *drifts inward, perches—the way sparrows*
> *do, waiting on consequence—and when silence*

*reclaims the air, is cautious. Changes
do not stop, but linger in the near edges*

*of dark, rumbling, braking. The flight of sparrows
traces rain, elongates the grey, changes
the shape of light and brings back silence,
like echo—quiet—in sedges,*

*rushes, reeds: The wetland changes
in the rain; marshwater stipples like sparrows
against a spotted sky—the edges
of light, the unpredictability of silence—*

*Bystanders hover, hunt for changes
in demeanour, for tell-tale flickers at the edges
of the mouth, shadow glances, sparrows
tracking the eyelids: The silence*

*cannot hold, again thunder edges
over the face, plain, peals changes,
treble, two, tenor, peals silence
like the afterwings of sparrows*

*when the night falls. The edges
of certainty blur: Silence
ripples, thunder murmurs on, changes
shadow into rain; the weight of sparrows*

*settles, and no-one moves: silence:
hollow and low—translating edges
into loss, the stroke of sparrows,
the gall of boglands. Grey day changes*

*how the bells toll: listen: how silence
endures grief, how whispering sparrows
first and last hunt the marshy edges
of remembrance: the rush, the ring of changes—*

ଛଏ

Quiet, and then
something stranger than the rush of wings:

the Merchant, who's been listening,
draws close: his fixed grin has cracked,

and as though he needed dispensation
to break from his own estate—

he asks to leave the Midway—

You seek peace, he says,
for the first time quietly:

*If I may,
I would join you—*

VI

CLOCK-FACE

When they pull away at last
from the Loop-the-loop and the Midway Fair,

they think they have finally outrun the fire-breath
that stalked them, the magic-men and spells—

yet still they forget memory, the ghost
wilderness they carry behind their eyes

that takes root in the fibrous tales they tell,
the parables and blessings, homilies, harangues,

the truths of blame and sentiment
that fill their days.

But while they talk, I listen,
hear them approaching, telling

of how, while time moves on outside
their noticing, they look in the long valleys

for where the moon rests, neighbourhood,
a place to dwell, a chance

to hear each other's stories,
sing each other's songs—

it is not so much a place
as a custom they must keep weaving,

not theirs to impose
but a rhythm to be learned, rain

in tune with the riverbed, pulse in accord
with hearts already home.

They're seeking meaning now, beyond
the surface of the world: seeking

the common sense of birch and wild blueberries,
of fossil tracks and spent shells—tumbling

closer, learning the force of indirection,
the power of being.

৵৶

The Woman knows. Many times
she stands apart, tending consequence and cure,

angelica for coughs and pennyroyal tea
for burning lungs,

snakeroot against fever,
cinquefoil stress.

She digs the roots they need to carry,
and hears the earth in undertones, while the Man

fixes his eyes on the changeable sky. *Time
follows us,* he mutters, holding on to a staff as he

limps towards a hill he does not recognize
and does not realize will one day be his last—

time follows us,

*strings of anecdote and pater noster, spiralling
thumbprints on the glass we no longer look for,
affirmation, denial—*

*We know that what's in front of us
is nothing, documentary
angled already towards conclusion—*

*it's narrative that lives,
tolled and retolled—*

Is the Boy awake? he asks, *he*

*needs to hear
this, Time
follows us—*

☙❧

Day by day the Boy learns something else,
digression, learns his father is imperfect,

because human,
and because human and imperfect,

wonderful,
and possible, in the course of time,

to hold close and start to leave:

I hear him, in another room,
reflecting:

we used to toss rings,
my father and I,
against a wall in a lower room:

he varied the rules—
throw the rings in turn,
one to nine,

or throw for the centre hook
and the highest total:
I didn't know

I was learning how to add,
or how to tether hand
and eye:

I thought I was
just with him:
and he with me—

I tell you this because, yes,
the Boy continues to grow—

not grow apart yet so much as
into himself,

which doesn't keep the rest from treating him
as if he were a stripling still,

intoning counsel like a peal of bells,
and they themselves still young.

The Waterwoman whispers riddles:

   stand on the bridge—
   the fish are returning upstream—
   every year the fish are returning
   red, upstream to spawn:

   black bear and kodiak
   stop at the creek's edge—
   stand on the bridge and you'll see them
   claw food from the stony creek:

   every year the bears
   fatten on salmon returning—the ospreys
   and bald eagles lift food from the river,
   they do not stand on the bridge:

> *the fish are returning*
> *upstream, ready to spawn*
> *in gravel shallows—they die*
> *giving back to the stony creek*
>
> *generation—stand on the bridge,*
> *you'll see them red and still,*
> *and rushing, flashing home*
> *the black of the rapids—*

The Merchant banters:

> *Thirteen or thirty-three,*
> *favour the wheel, never free—*
>
> *Ride the clock if you truly dare—*
> *but no-one is free who dallies at fair—*

The Boy's Mother is more direct: she fastens
on the hem of the quilt she has been mending,

and also on her son: *Remember the Fair?* she asks,
not really asking—*The produce halls where you*

sampled food you thought was free? Did you ever
look around? with care? What else did you take in?

> *They used to wear hats,*
> *the farm wives who manned the cookery tables.*

Prepared for anything they were,
hard lives written beside their eyes,
hatpins and half-smiles readied for town—

In front of them they'd spread the labours of summer and
  early fall:
jars of Lamberts, sun still glinting off the ripe fruit,
  loganberry jam,
tableaus of butterscotch glazed in meringue—

Truth be told (birthing calves, daubing stain, switching
  the herd home,
churning), they ran the whole farm as much as the men
  who every year
gruffed costs and rain and paraded bulls in the cattle
  hall. Their children
were used to the facts of life, if never the speed. Remember
  this.

No reason to regret what hasn't changed, what has. Nothing
superior about drawn eyes and inarticulate gingham.

Those birdsquat hats, though,
and the fierce hatpins:
they said don't judge by what you think you see—

you'd have been a fool not to have listened, and distrust
the ribbons,
the blue rosettes—

Promises, the Boy mumbles,
I still don't understand:

*Every spring I feel new heat in the earth,
see apple buds, scudding clouds,
hear gossip in the offing—*

*the girl who lives the next valley over
circles by as though on wheels, shoots
past me, faster each time—*

*and just when I think I know what to say,
some unexpected spoke in the universe
trips my tongue—I live*

an elongated winter: what must I do?

*I bleed inside, watching,
while the girl goes on to tilt and disappear—*

Mushrooms, the Landsman interrupts, impatiently—
Take mushrooms:

*after any heavy rain, fungus:
but there's little romance
in technocrats
declaring why:* spore
and a sudden dose of extra
nitrogen:

*no wonder the old ones
called them* fairy rings,
and stayed up nights with clumsy

registers—spirit-hunters
hoping to catch the little people
dancing:

earlier still—promise of treasure
be damned—you wouldn't have caught
anyone with any sense stepping inside
those circles: that innocent-looking
overnight line of toadstools
signified:

souls of the dead, *they said,*
come back to blame—or maybe bless—
you couldn't take the chance which,
so stood apart—
maybe even breath of the dragon
clawing the night—

witches' curses, sorcerers' brew,
the blasted site where the devil
rests his milk churn—*good to have*
names for something to fear:
or something to frighten others with—
the bald facts of power:

threaten the young with doom and
the devil, they'll go on singing:
threaten them with impotence
and curdled milk,
they just might listen,
say the crones:

*in the north country, courting villagers
used to throw toadstools into bonfires
on midsummer's eve*—kept evil spirits away,
they said—and brought young folk
close together, *dancing dark
and the longest day—*

Silence.

The Boy still listens, but more than ever now,
he poses questions they can't quite answer.

His father tries:

*Open a ringbox, you look for the future,
expect to find promise, nimbus,
corona, hope—perhaps a red trinket,
the sum of all answers, maybe the moon—*

*you can snap the ringbox shut
and think you've already caught the gold ring:
yes, and circuses, and maybe you have,
though you won't be sure*

until later corrals you, across the river—

But the Boy shrugs, rejoining,

What then, riding geometry:
can you ever choose?

VII

RINGBOX

You could maybe guess what happens next,
or I could tell you lies: I could say

> *Everyone lives happily ever after,* or
> *One of them dies a gruesome death in*

> *dragonfire,* or

> *Coils catch them,* or

> *Slowly they waste away*
> *from carelessness and lavender,*

but none of these is true.

They live for years,
until.

❧ ☙

All stories travel along
a ring road of the mind,

from *Once* and *Then*
to the lip of *Until.*

Or touch it many times, call it
fairground, desert, dragon, war,

marriage, birth, or riverwater:

something that stops, alters,
reaches farther into the hills.

Yes.

This town was along the Travellers' way:
it's where we met at last,

by the rope-makers' gate,

though they pushed on,
and I remained,

sotted,
stalled in the apple shade.

No matter now. Regret

is not for the strong. I try
not to regret.

It was late on a burnt August day
when the Travellers walked out of my dreaming

and down from the Western hills,
along that line of poplars you can

still mark there, the road never straight,
and dust stirring then as now

in the sorghum fields.

I knew who they were, recognized them
instantly from voice and quarrel,

and what they wore: paper rainbows,
mottled skins; the little Gambler

striped in distraction, the Landsman
giant in houndstooth brown. I saw

the Woman who cloaked herself in memory
and leaf; the Boy who was wrapped in promise;

the Merchant glittering mirrorglass; the magpie
Actor, red and gold—

and trailing after the others, the Woman's Friend,
clothed head to toe in smoke so dark it rippled,

black as footprints,
silent as the hour she was born.

Safety, they say to me, *safety—*
Where is the moon?

I give them apples.

It is not enough.

They pause by the smouldering coals but
do not rest, their stories lashing at shadow speed:

all night they tell their chronicle—firedeath and
underland, waterbirth and stars—nothing

stops them, not watchman's calls nor maggot cold
nor hunger fleering, crawling through the brain:

we share bread, ale,
a circle of stones:

it is not enough:

they leave without formalities
before the first bells ring the sunrise.

Had I not slept, had I not turned away,
I could have gone along—

Oh, I could tell you other tales—
about sellers of gravity, contraband

and the nearness of the dark.
I've met wild-eyed magicians and conjurors

of privilege, been dazzled by women and
spun into circus rage—and punished, yes, left

alleyside in rope and rags, and
tempted by ladders that climb the sky—

I, too, once had a father—

I prefer the tales the Travellers tell
to the size of revolutions:

> *Do what you will,* they whisper—

> *befriend the moon, count crescent bells,*
> *or cycle Saturn's aureoles—*

> But read the earth:

> *the road has wings:*

> *do not mistake the sequence*
> *for the season.*

The Keeper of the keys then murmurs *Yes*,
his voice as edged as ocean.

In *Pali*, he begins:

the word is dhamma,
translated generally as natural law,
the real: alas, too open to mis-hearing.

Try the way of the higher truth,
though if you have a scoffing inclination,
mountaintop old saws will come to mind,
which go against intent.

Try right duty, virtuous conduct,
path to personal liberation
as you take your part in the cycle of life.

Perhaps. One of the texts is called
the Book of Seven.
Dhamma. *Or Sanskrit* Dharma,
from dhri, *'manner of being.'*

Suppose we greeted one another, What is
your manner of being? *and listened past disguise.*

Suppose we heard the answer ring seven times seven,
as though the mountains sang it, rivers, eagles, trees:
I am a child living, borne and real—

dragonwings might sing us home—

But I, the Boy declares,
finding a voice as he grows,

I've not yet lived:

my home is not from then
but still before me—home

is what I have not seen:

climbing the black-bear mountains, playing
shadow tag in a thousand towns—I want to

walk beyond the edge of north, learn
every song of riverbank and barley:

I would do more—I would go on—I would
remember what it is I do not know—

ھ ھ

The Boy's preoccupied, and the
Waterwoman's dreaming rapids

when the Travellers pause by a braided stream:

the Keeper reads, the Actor plays the pipes,
the Merchant fishes, the Gambler counts

riverstones—and when the Man reaches out
to hold the Woman's hand,

even the giant Landsman settles back,
breathing slow and smiling,

> *summer, like a lover's knot,*
> *ties us in daisies,*
> *eyes open, stems green—*
>
> *like a lover's knot, eyes*
> *open, summer befriends us,*
> *philadelphus, syringa, snowpetal daze—*
>
> *eyes open, like summer,*
> *syringa mocks us, but gently,*
> *weds us to oranges, stammering sweet—*
>
> *gently, like blood, mock orange*
> *opens, teases the summer, stumbling lovers,*
> *lingering green in fumbles of snow—*

৩৵

So another season passes, red leaf and sooty bracken,
ice-petal, frond—

and yes, the Boy is growing up and
now growing away, as his Mother knows,

and as his father, once young, and suddenly old,
begins to begin to die.

The Woman stokes the fire that keeps
the Old Man warm, sits by his bedside,

works on the quilt she had started long ago:

> *ring-pattern:*
> *hilling pantlegs and pinafores,*
> *apron scraps from the airing cupboard,*
> *torn linens, fringes,*
>
> *poring over them, hearing the offspring still,*
> *then and then,*
> *the bickering, hollering, deafening, posturing:*
>
> *weathering the anger, the blistering truth,*
> *the liquoring up and motoring off, suffering:*
> *conjuring laughter out of the fracturing melee, answering*
> *love, with love:*
>
> *but all the sauntering days as well, colouring*
> *over the lines and into difference,*
> *vinegar and sugar,*
>
> *sewing them back together, after they're gone,*
> *picturing what is, what might have been*
> *or come again,*
> *hankering after meaning,*

  caring enough to remember well,
  daring to cut memory into flowerbeds,
  covering

 ❦

It does not take long, looking back—
a gate, a bridge, a glimmer, gone—

for the last days to tumble past pain
and into *After*.

When the Boy recalls the time,
he lifts his father out of anonymity at last,

naming him
with affection and wonder:

  what are you doing here, *my father asked*
  when I showed up at the bedside.

  don't worry him, *they'd said to me*
  after I'd come back from across the water.

  as if, I thought, just by being here,
  I could avoid it.

or earlier, when they'd rung from home
on the only-if-you-have-to line, and said

don't worry but, a cautionary start,
your father's had a coronary, blunt, and then

he should recover, but if you're going to come,
come.   now.

that tangle of possibilities. the pause.
real and implied.

no answer but the only.
why are you here.

decades on, I hear it again,
this boxing ring of silences—the saying, the unsaid.

healing the heart, I wanted to shout.
maybe my own.

but could not even whisper, until
later, when maybe the old man could not hear.

though he knew, just as I knew,
the dimensions of his dance with quiet.

in my eyes he wore coronet and laurel,
his hours absorbed in drafting pathways.

now, what are you doing here.
a challenge, not a question. quiet:

but silly bugger, *he had snapped once,*
at a young man who'd hurt. why
are we here. because of anger.
because of love.

☙❧

The Old Man's last words were not
just for him, he knows. But to hear them

was to bring back their long wandering,
the arid road, the ring they'd followed,

watercourses
and the book of sevens.

It all comes down to this, he'd said—

I heard him too—

   a little pond

   and a copper sundown.

Night, he'd said,

his breath halting,
his dark eyes drifting grey,

    night gathers on the lake
    the way afterthoughts mutter
    should've said and *grind slow,*
    while just out of reach, light

    tips the spruce, the dying pines:
    night gathers on the lake:
    kingfishers circle to nest,
    the rapid skroak, *the loons' hollow*

    codas quiet, till next morning
    reclaims the spruce, the dying pines,
    and fishing starts again—life
    is conditional here, drought depleting

    the water, beetles killing the trees:
    next morning's words are codas,
    conversations out of kilter—
    except, this night, trout rise

    to a cloud of evening insects, midges,
    mosquitoes—the beetles killing the trees
    consume the light, but dragonflies
    dart and hover, dart and hover:

    in the brief space between lake and sky—
    as afterthoughts startle, when trout
    flick stars at midge and evening,
    and lilypads mimic the moon—light,

in fragments, ricochets in rings—

❧

Those who congregate to listen
pause for a moment,

a few linger, a few turn away—
and those who *can* move on

move on: they pick up books and satchels,
hammers, matches, clay waterjugs and powdered

snakeroot, panpipes, amber appleseed,
and they step again into living—

though the Boy (a Man now, with friends, lover,
dragontrack and secret name, fair to stumble up against

and riverground to reach for) turns back often,
especially when frost glazes the windowpane,

to remember:

> *what remains of the family*
> *sits around the supper table*
>
> *talking loss: absent friends,*
> *says one, lifting a glass,*

*and those who have gone away,
may they somewhere find
the happiness they've longed for—*

*the circle forms, is broken,
tries to form again, memory
ghosting the vacant chairs:*

*those who have come together
interrupt their emptiness:*

*on a clear night, everyone
looks for a crescent moon—*

֍

Go now.
The tale is done, until.

֍

Who am I, *you ask?*
Only one who hears tales

when the moon disappears
and the wind rises like a cloud of wings.

I am you, or the one beside you,
a rope-maker under an apple tree,

with a basket near me, and a tangle inside
of hope and fear—

The river does not rest,
and the bell above the east gate is ringing—

Telling Words

I am indebted to many circles of friends for companionship and conversation, and for ideas and images that have threaded their way into this book. I especially want to thank Sherrill and John Grace, for their enthusiastic appreciation of the Ring Cycle, which set me on a separate journey; Jack and Dianne Hodgins, for glimpses of remembered childhood, which led me back to Quadra Street and north of 49th Avenue; Ross and Gisela Labrie, for summer days spent at Little Pressy Pond in the Cariboo; Ron and Pat Smith and Hiro Boga, at Oolichan, for editorial guidance and for spirited talk about philosophies of number and the quest for words; Jane Flick and Bob Heidbreder, for their enthusiastic delight in language; Laurie Ricou, for his quiet wit and his dialogues with ecology in *Salal* and *Invader Species*; Michael Ondaatje, for memories of an elephant ride in Amber and for the mysteries of *The Story*; Clark Blaise, Bharati Mukherjee, and the late Eli Mandel, for tales told on that same trip around India; my squash partners, over forty years, for their acrobatic play with deception and disguise; and all others who tell stories with laughter and love.

૭≫ ≪૭

Motifs intertwine in *The Rope-maker's Tale*—rings and numbers, for instance, and rounds of various kinds, from games and songs to fairgrounds and cycles of nature.

They tell tales inside tales, about hope, greed, discord, loss, persistence, happiness, the moveable boundaries of desire. And about completeness, which in numerous cultural histories is linked with the number 7 (Old English *sēofon*, Aramaic *shib-aw*). Yet even the idea of fullness or completeness, when it crosses boundaries, can change meaning.

Words, too, shift shape and gather resonance—whether by history and definition (*ring, round, circus, coronary*) or through structure, sound, and association—as with the words *dragon* and *dragoon* [from L. *draco*, serpent] and *dragonfly* [the predatory 'darning-needle,' order Odonata, meaning 'toothed ones'], which overlap indirectly and aurally with the words *draft, draught, draw, drag* [all from OE *dragan*] and *dragoman*, the guide [from Arabic *tarjumān*, translator], whose role in story-telling is always more than neutral.

Perhaps the real point about stories is that they can never be complete, but aspire always to circle into other stories, to be passages, during which we are invited to listen to the world.

W. H. New is the author of a wide range of books, including several books for children, the *Encyclopedia of Literature in Canada*, *Underwood Log* (shortlisted for the Governor General's Award for Poetry), and *Along a Snake Fence Riding*.

His writing has received international recognition, including the Lorne Pierce Medal and the Governor General's International Award in Canadian Studies. He was appointed an Officer of the Order of Canada in 2006. *The Rope-Maker's Tale* is his ninth book of poetry.